Denver Travel Guide

Sightseeing, Hotel, Restaurant & Shopping Highlights

Richard Wright

Table of Contents

Denver

Denver, the capital of Colorado, is nicknamed the Mile High City at 5,280 feet (1 mile) above sea level in the Rocky Mountains. The city's neighborhoods include LoDo (Lower Downtown), Capitol Hill, Highland, Washington Park, Baker and Lowry. With its green city parklands, the impressive Rocky Mountains as a backdrop and the nonstop urban day and nightlife, Denver is a hub of activity that is sure to thrill the visitor.

The largest city in Colorado is located just to the east of the Front Range of the Rocky Mountains and west of the High Plains. This makes the city mostly flat to the west side and hilly throughout the rest.

Denver has over 80 neighborhoods and more than 200 green parks to enjoy on a sunny, clear day. These parks are often the focal points of the neighborhoods. City Park is the largest park in Denver and is 314 acres in size. Denver has more than 4,000 acres of parks plus an additional 14,000 acres of mountain parks.

Culture

With a large Hispanic population, Denver hosts some major Mexican-American celebrations. In May there is a large Cinco de Mayo festival that attracts over 500,000 people. In September visit the El Grito de la Independcia, the celebration of Mexican Independence. Denver also hosts the Lowrider festival and the Dia De Los Muertos art show. At these events or on a regular trip try Denver's famous Southwestern cuisine.

With Denver being so close to the mountains many visitors spend their time taking advantage of the beautiful natural environment. The winter weekends are often filled with people skiing in the mountains to the west of Denver. In the warmer months vistors will enjoy hiking or climbing in the mountains. Many take advantage of the location to go kayaking or camping.

Asian-American festivals are popular in Denver. The Chinese New Year has a large celebration. The Dragon Boat festival is in July. September is when locals host the Moon Festival. Denver also has two Chinese newspapers.

Denver is the setting for some well-known television shows. The show Dynasty was set in Denver. The Bill Engvall Show which stared comedian Bill Engvall was set in Denver though it was filmed in Los Angeles. The Disney Channel currently has a show which is set in Denver called Good Luck Charlie. It is also where the show E-Vet Interns takes place. The ABC original show starring Tim Allen is set in Denver as is the ABC Family series Make it or Break it.

Location & Orientation

Denver is nestled between the great Rocky Mountains to its west and the High Plains to its east. With only being a few miles from the Front Range of the Rocky Mountains Denver is a very hilly city. It is also the most populated city in Colorado and indeed is the most populous city within a 500 mile radius.

With Denver being so large it is made up of eighty neighborhoods. Some of the more well-known neighborhoods are the historical and trendy LoDo. This neighborhood is made up of a little more than a 23 square block radius that was the original location of Denver.

Another well-known neighborhood is Highland which is in north Denver. This is one of the most sought after areas to live in Denver with its proximity to LoDo making it appealing. Capitol Hill is where the artists and bohemians hang out. It is a place filled with galleries, bars, clubs, and restaurants. With two concert venues the neighborhood is also known for having a wild nightlife. With the gay pride parade going through the neighborhood every year the neighborhood has also been called the gay village.

Denver has many bicycle commuters and many streets have bicycle lanes. When you add this to the over 850 miles of paved bike paths you can see why Denver is so bicycle friendly. The city even started a Bicycle program where for a small fee people can check out a bicycle, much like a library allows you to check out a book. You can rent for 24 hours, 7 days, 30 days, or one year. The cost of membership depends on how long you want to ride the bicycle. This will make it easier for those people who are on vacation who want to use a bike.

The public transportation is operated by Regional Transportation District (RTD). The RTD have over 1,000 buses. These buses cover 38 districts that are in 8 different counties. They are also putting into effect FasTracks which will soon give commuters the opportunity to travel by train. FasTracks hopes to be up and running before 2016.

Climate & When to Visit

Denver has four distinct seasons and with Denver being located so close to the Rocky Mountains it can have sudden changes in weather. The warmest month of the year for Denver is July with the average temperature being 90 degrees Fahrenheit (32 degrees Celsius) and the average low being 60 degrees Fahrenheit (16 degrees Celsius). December is the coldest month with highs only reaching 44 degrees Fahrenheit (7 degrees Celsius) and the low falling 18 degrees Fahrenheit (-8 degrees Celsius). The average first snowfall is October 18 and the last snowfall averages around April 30. Denver actually has 300 days of sunshine.

With all the different festivals that Denver hosts you can go at any time of the year and enjoy it. Though many like to take advantage of the closeness of the mountains. If hiking, camping, climbing or kayaking are what you are looking for then travel to Denver in late spring or during the summer. If you are wanting to ski then the winter months are for you.

Sightseeing Highlights

City Park

City Park is the largest park in Denver and is 330 acres in
size located in east-central Denver. City Park has at two
lakes; Ferril Lake and Duck Lake and also a boathouse.
The two biggest attractions that City Park features are the
Denver Zoo and the Denver Museum of Nature and
Science which makes it a great way to spend the day rain
or shine.

Denver Zoo is on over 80 acres of land inside City Park. There is a bicycle kiosk at the zoo entrance so you can choose to bike your way through if you want. This zoo is open 365 days out of the year and there are almost 4,000 animals to be seen. These animals are from 700 different species which means that you can see animals here that you would not see in other zoos. Admission price runs anywhere from free to $15. The zoo also offers free days, you can check the website to see if there is a free day when you plan to visit Denver. In the summer months admission to the zoo is open from 9am to 5pm with the grounds staying open until 6pm. Should you choose to go in the winter months admission is open from 10 am to 4pm with the grounds staying open until 5pm.

Shows and exhibits are scheduled throughout the day. At 10am and 2:30 pm you can catch the Sea Lion Show. Then at 10:45am and again at 2pm is the Toyota Elephant Passage Demonstration. Also at 2pm is Africa's Greatest Predators. Tropical Discovery and Bird World is open from 10am to 5pm. Outside of Bird World at 10:15am and 3:30 pm is African Penguin Feeding. If you want to see the Lorikeet Adventure then plan your visit for the weekend. It is from 10am to 3:30 pm Friday, Saturday and Sunday. If you have children they will enjoy the carousel ride and the train.

For more information about the Denver Zoo you feel free to stop by their website. http://www.denverzoo.org/

The other major attraction at City Park is the Denver Museum of Nature and Science which was established in 1900. This museum is open every day of the year except December 25 from 9am to 5pm. Admission prices vary depending on what part of the museum you want to see. You can check admission prices here http://www.dmns.org/plan-your-visit/ticket-prices/.

There are several current exhibitions at the museum and some rotating ones. By checking the museum's website you can see which exhibits will be available when you visit. Expedition Health is a place where you not only learn about the human body but you learn about your own body. This exhibit allows you to examine some of your own cells, it is an interactive exhibit. Space Odyssey is a unique exhibit since it lets you see things as they would be seen from outer space. Egyptian Mummies, Gems and Minerals, North American Indian Culture, and Wildlife exhibits are all ones that are among the permanent collection.

You can catch shows at the Planetarium and the IMAX. If you get hungry stop by the T-Rex Café or Grab & Go. For more information on the Denver Museum of nature and Science feel free to stop by the website http://www.dmns.org/ or call 303.370.6000. It is located in City Park at 2001 Colorado Blvd.

Denver Art Museum

The Denver Art Museum is located at 100 W. 14th Ave. Parkway in Denver. This museum is open from 10am to 5pm Tuesday through Thursday, Saturday and Sunday. On Friday the hours are from 10am to 8pm. Mondays it is closed. On the first Saturday of every month admission is free. Admission price ranges from free (0-5 years old) to $13.

There are always new exhibits rotating at the museum and there are 13 permanent collections. These include African Art, American Indian Art, Architecture Design & Graphics, Asian Art, European and American Art, the Logan Collection, Modern and Contemporary Art, Oceanic Art, Photography, Pre-Columbian Art, Spanish Colonial Art, Textile Art, and Western American Art. These exhibits are sure to please any art lover.

For the visitors with children there are daily activities. Just for Fun Center is a place where children can try on costumes and play with color. There are more children friendly activities but they are not always offered. It is best to check the website at http://www.denverartmuseum.org/.

LoDo District

The LoDo (Lower Downtown) district is the historical part of Denver and is located where Denver was originally built. It is now a trendy place to visit and live. It has 90 brewpubs, sports bars, rooftop cafes and restaurants. LoDo also has some terrific shops. If you are interested in the history of Denver then maybe a walking tour is for you. On this guided tour you can learn about the history of the buildings and which buildings were used to house the local saloons, brothels, and the people who owned them. To schedule a walking tour of LoDo visit its website http://www.lodo.org/.

Colorado Railroad Museum

The Colorado Railroad Museum is worth the 25 minute drive to Golden, Colorado. It is located at 17155 West 44th Avenue in Golden, Colorado. This unique museum is one that every train lover will enjoy. The locomotives are not just for looking at, they are operational. Not only can you look at these trains but you can also go for a ride. On most Saturdays you can go for a ride on the 1/3 mile track which will give you a different view of the roundhouse and turntable. Like model trains then stop by the train garden or check out the Denver HO Society model railroad which is located on the lower level of the main building. Here the layout is much like the railroads of historical Colorado.

These trains are operated by a member of the Denver HO Society on Tuesdays. If you have a little one who adores Thomas the Train then check the website to see if Day Out With Thomas is going on when you will be in the Denver area. Check out the website to see if there are any special events going on when you plan your visit http://coloradorailroadmuseum.org/. Admission ranges from free to $10. If you have a family then check out the family admission rate of $30 which covers two adults and up to five children under the age of 16. The museum is open from 9am to 5pm year round with special holiday hours on Easter, Christmas Eve, and New Year's Eve. They are closed Christmas day, New Year's Day and Thanksgiving.

Echo Lake & Mount Evans

Mount Evans is called "the road to the stars" as it is the highest paved automobile road in America. Drive the 14 miles to the Mount Evans summit parking lot. Once there you can hike ¼ mile to the top of Mount Evans. Mount Evans is 14,264 feet high and telling your friends that you climbed that mountain would impress. The road to the top of Mount Evans starts at Echo Lake. This beautiful mountain lake is known as a great fishing spot. A trail going around the lake is ¾ of a mile long. There are some beautiful picnic grounds near the lake. The road is closed from October to May due to snow.

You can still hike, bike, or even snow-shoe along trails. If you want to stay overnight there are several campgrounds at different elevations. Access fees for motorized vehicles depend on the number of passengers. The access pass is good for 3 days. The fees can go as high as $40. For more information and to see if the road is open at the time of your visit please stop by the website http://www.mountevans.com/index.html.

Georgetown

Georgetown is 42 miles west of Denver but worth the drive. Georgetown started out as a mining camp in 1859. Once popular because of its potential to make you rich it is now popular because of its location. It has beautiful views of the Rocky Mountains. No matter what your interests you will be able to find something to do in Georgetown. In the winter months there is ice fishing, ice racing; for those of you who enjoy ice skating you can do that at Werlin Park. There is always skiing and snowboarding.

The warmer months are filled with activities. Spend the day relaxing while fishing at Georgetown Lake. The lake is stocked with trout, rainbows, Brookes, and browns. There are limits on the size and number of fish so be sure to check out Georgetown's website if fishing will be on your agenda. Travel the old mining trails on ATVs with the Mountains ATV Tours. Visit in June and you can participate in the Slacker Half Marathon Races. These races are all downhill and proceeds go to local charities. Whitewater rafting can be done at two locations Arkansas River and Clear Creek.

A day and evening of leisure can be found in Georgetown, perfect for a romantic date or to enjoy with friends and family. Start your day off with a Victorian Garden Tour where several historic homes are opened to you so you can see what life was like during the early years of the mining town. Then from 10am to 6pm you can stop by Canyon Wind Cellars for winetasting. Taste several different wines or enjoy a glass of your favorite along with a cheese plate. Next, top your evening off with a night at the opera at The Central City Opera House. This is a beautifully restored theatre that will be well worth the drive. It is around 30 minutes from Georgetown, at least it is on its way back to Denver with only a slight detour.

Georgetown has 3 museums. Stop by the Hotel De Paris Museum will send you back in time to 1875. The Hammil House Museum is a magnificent example of a Country Style Gothic Revival house. The Georgetown Electric Museum is an operating hydroelectric plant that was built in 1900.

Don't forget to take advantage of the Georgetown Loop Railroad. These open passenger cars pulled by a steam locomotive give you a wonderful view of the mountains and gold/silver mines while you are on your way up the canyon to Silver Plume.

To find out about more of any of these activities check out Georgetown's website. You may want to plan on spending an entire day here. http://www.georgetown-colorado.org/main.htm

Confluence Park

Confluence Park is where Denver was originally founded as a mining camp in 1858. Now it is the center of Denver's 850 mile bike trail way. This park in downtown Denver is located next to the South Platte River and Cherry Creek. There is a large outdoor amphitheater for park concerts. With a nice beach and plenty of green space this park is perfect for picnics. You can go kayaking on the Platte River. If you want to see fire performers and drummers practice fire spinning by the water then you want to head to the Confluence Park on a warm Tuesday or Friday night.

Cherokee Ranch & Castle Foundation

The Cherokee Ranch and Castle Foundation is located outside of Denver in Sedalia. The 1450s Scottish style castle was built by the Johnson family in 1924. They later sold their homestead to Tweet Kimball in 1954, he also purchased the neighboring homestead and combined the two.

The castle holds several performances a year. Some types of performances are murder-mystery, theatrical, jazz, classical, family, and special performances. The website has a calendar that can be checked for performances. If you want a guided tour they are $15 per person and offered for kids (fourth grade and older) and adults on Wednesdays, Thursdays, and Saturdays. These are typically an hour and a half long. While on the tour you will hear about the history of the castle, the people who built it and inhabited it, you will see its collection of art form around the world and the unique furnishing that fill the castle.

Ever wanted tea in a castle? Now is your chance. Tea is again offered to those in fourth grade or older. The cost is $42 per person. There is a seasonal menu. Of course you will get scones with clotted cream and jam, finger sandwiches, and pastries. Tea is served every other Wednesday or Saturday from 2pm to 4pm. You can also request a private tea for birthdays, bridal showers, or just outings with your friends or family.

The castle also offers hikes, whisky tasting, summer camps for adults and children alike. To find out more about these check out their website for the newest schedule.

303-688-5555
6113 Daniels Park Rd.
Sedalia, 80135
http://www.cherokeeranch.org/

Dinosaur Ridge

Want a fun and educational experience? Visit Dinosaur Ridge and see the creatures who use to roam Colorado. Hike the Dinosaur Ridge trail way, this hike will take anywhere from 1 to 2 hours. Along the way stop at up to 15 different spots of interest. These spots include fossils, scenic overlooks, and interesting rock formations. At the Dinosaur Ridge Track site you can see actual fossilized dinosaur tracks. You can also learn more about it at the Trek Through Time exhibit. Want to touch a dinosaur bone then head over to the Bone Quarry where you will find dinosaur bones fossilized in rock.

Walking the gravel Triceratops Trail you will see 3-D triceratops footprints. This trail is a little harder to walk and not likely passable for those who are disabled. Not only will you see footprints on this trail but you will see fossils of plants imbedded into the rock.

Backyard Bones: Dinosaur Dig Pit is perfect for younger ones. It allows children to dig much like a paleontologist would. They will discover bones and then investigate to find out why the dinosaur they found was there.

Trek Through Time Dinosaur Exhibit Hall is a place where you can go to discover even more about dinosaurs. The Cost is only $2 per person, three and younger get in for free. Here you will find five murals, fossils that have been dug up and placed behind glass to keep them safe, and interactive exhibits. If you get hungry during your visit stop by The Stegosaurus Snack Shack which is located next to the gift shop. For more information and to check for special events, dates and times that these areas are open check out the website.

303-697-3466
16831 W. Alameda Pkwy
Morrison, 80465
http://www.dinoridge.org/index.html

Museum of Denver

The Children's Museum of Denver is open from 9am to 4pm, Monday through Friday; staying open until 7pm on Wednesdays. Saturday and Sunday you can come play from 10am to 5pm. Admission ranges from $7 to $9. This is a place where children can play and learn at the same time. There are 15 playscapes all of which are designed to be fun for everyone though they have target age groups.

3,2,1…Blast Off! This is a wonderful place for a young, aspiring astronaut. Here children can build their own rockets and launch them. They can also view a video of real rocket launches. The wind tunnel is a place where the children can place different colored scarves to see how the wind moves them. This is fun for all though it was designed with those between the ages of 2 and 8 in mind.

Bubbles is a playscape where children will learn about shapes, mixtures, force, and evaporation. They will use not only their large and fine motor skills but will use mathematics and science. At the Big Bubble Maker you can make bubbles that are over 6 feet long! The Drop Zone is where you can pop vapor-filled bubbles. You can fill bubbles with vapor mist at the Vapor Station. There are so many more wonderful things to do and explore in this playscape. This is for all ages but the educational aspect of it is geared towards those 6 to 8 years of age.

Just Add Water is a fun water exhibit where you will get wet. It is a good idea to have a towel handy or even clothes that will dry quickly. This water exhibit is not a place or swimming, it is a place for learning and having fun. Here children will learn about geysers, whirlpools and fountains. Here children can work pumps, they can channel, and they can sprinkle water. They can even paint with it. The target age group is 1 t 8 but this would be fun for all especially on a hot day.

Spotlights is where you can explore color and movement. When you step onto the floor you immediately get a colored spotlight that follows you around when you move. Your color stays the same, other people on the floor will have other colors. When you get close to someone your circles will combine and the colors will blend. Learn how two colors can make a new color in this fun interactive exhibit.

The Art Studio is designed for those who are between the ages of 2 and 4 though it will be fun for anyone. Here is a place where children can explore their creative side. Let them grab an easel and paint. There are many different types of crafts that can be done here.

The Assembly Plant is targeted for those 4 to 8 years of age. This playscape provides you and your child with all the tools and recyclable materials that you will need to create a new masterpiece. Get settled in a station where you can have your own blueprint. Here using the tools will help children with their fine motor skills. If they choose to follow a blueprint then they will have to read and follow the directions.

The Big Backyard is designed for those who are 3 to 6 but again this is something that will be fun for everyone. This oversized backyard will let children see the outside world from the point of view of the creatures who live outside. Let them explore the world of an ant or that of a bird with the costumes that the kids can wear.

Click Clack Train Track will be fun experience for all but it is targeted to 2 to 5 year olds. Here they can put on a conductors hat and build train tracks. Watch your little engineer build a landscape around the train tracks by setting up trees. This will be fun for any child who enjoys trains.

Fire Station No. 1 is a wonderful firefighter experience designed to engage those 3 to 6 years of age. Allow your little one to dress up as a fire fighter, get in a fire truck and learn about what it takes to be one of these heroes. This exhibit is pretty much a recreation of a firehouse. The children can see a firefighter's bunk and kitchen, see how they live when they have to stay at the firehouse. Along with the 911 dispatch station there is the always fun fireman's pole. Your children are sure to enjoy this exhibit, when they are tired out from all the playing sit down and look through the fireman's yearbook to see a history of this brave profession.

While you are at the Children's Museum of Denver do not forget to stop by these other playstations Kinetics where you can experience a life size marble run and Hopscotch where you can draw on a statue of a cow or lay hopscotch with the family.

303-433-7444
2121 Children's Museum Dr.
Denver, 80211
http://www.mychildsmuseum.org/Default.aspx

Recommendations for the Budget Traveler

Places to Stay

Residence Inn Denver City Center

1724 Champa Street
Denver, CO
(303) 296-3444
http://www.marriott.com/hotels/travel/denrd-residence-inn-denver-city-center/

This hotel has a great location as it is within walking distance of many shops, restaurants, entertainment, arts, and sporting events. This hotel rooms feature full suites. Check in is at 4pm and check out is at 11am. There is parking for an extra $25 a day. Take advantage of the complimentary hot buffet style breakfast, room delivery of meals from local restaurants and the Bar-B-Q/ picnic area. Each room offers wired and wireless internet. In the evenings there is complimentary beer and wine.

All of the rooms offer air conditioning, iron and ironing board, cable television, coffee/tea service, bottle water (for a fee), the bathroom has a hair dryer. The biggest thing that each room has is a kitchen that is fully equipped with what you would need to cook. The hotel offers grocery delivery for a fee.

Prices start at $199 a night which gives you a queen bed and a sofa bed. The rates go as high as $319 a night which gives you a 2 room suite; two bedrooms with queen size beds, a sofa bed, and two bathrooms.

Holiday Inn Express Denver Aurora-Medical Center

1500 South Abilene Street
Aurora, Colorado
(303) 369-8400
http://www.ihg.com/holidayinnexpress/hotels/us/en/aurora/denac/hoteldetail

Only 20 minutes from the Denver International Airport and less than 30 minutes away from LoDo this hotel is in a great location. You can catch a sporting event or go shopping in LoDo. They offer a complimentary hot breakfast. Though there is no restaurant in the hotel there are several restaurants nearby. There is an on-site fitness center and an outdoor pool. Each room offers cable television, pay-per-view movies, in room video games are available, and kitchenette. There is a work desk and high-speed internet access. The room rates start at low as $79 a night.

Warwick Hotel

1776 Grant Street
Denver, Colorado
(303) 861-2000
http://www.warwickdenver.com/

This hotel luxurious hotel is located on the edges of the Uptown and Capitol Hill neighborhoods. This puts it away from the noise but still close enough that you do not have to travel far to get to great restaurants, shopping, and clubs. The hotel offers many amenities including Randolph's Restaurant and Bar. Take advantage of the heated rooftop pool. You can even check out the gift shop. The hotel offers high-speed internet access. There is a fitness center, same day laundry service, and 24 hour room service.

The rooms offer wireless or wired internet access, 32 inch televisions, cable with HBO, honor bar, floor to ceiling glass doors to the balcony, and balcony furniture. There are robes and slippers in the rooms. All of this for a price starting at $129 a night.

Embassy Suites, Downtown & Convention Center

1420 Stout Street
Denver, Colorado
(303) 592-1000
http://embassysuites3.hilton.com/en/hotels/colorado/e
mbassy-suites-denver-downtown-convention-center-
DENESES/index.html

This hotel is within walking distance of downtown. You are close to the attractions of downtown Denver when staying here. It is close to the 16th Street Mall and the Theatrical District. Some of the great things this hotel offers are the indoor pool and fitness center. Looking for a place to relax but not wanting to go to your room yet? Check out the hotel bar and lounge.

Each room has a private bedroom and a living room. Enjoy the microwave, wet bar, fridge, and the two televisions that are in every suite. Each suite has internet access, a desk, air conditioning, a complimentary paper on weekdays, and pay per view movies. Cribs and toddler beds are available upon request.

Rates start as low as $99 a night. If you want a room with a mountain view be prepared to pay a little more.

Magnolia Hotel

818 17th Street
Denver, Colorado
(303) 607-9000
http://www.magnoliahotels.com/denver/magnolia-hotel-denver.php

This hotel is in a historic bank building. It is only a block away from the 16th Street Mall. Summit County's four ski areas are an hour drive away. This makes it a great location for those who have come to Denver to enjoy the slopes. There are some wonderful room amenities. High speed internet access, flat screen television, pay-per-view movies and Nintendo, in room coffee and tea, and bathrobes. Eat in the Lounge, at Harry's Bar or order in room service. Rates start as low as $129 a night.

Places to Eat & Drink

Bang!

3472 West 32nd Street
Denver, Colorado
(303) 455-1117
http://bangdenver.com/

This restaurant serves high quality dishes without the high price tag. Instead of an open kitchen the kitchen has a street view. The cooks are on display for everyone to see.

The menu here changes two to three times a year. Here you will find comfort food with Southern flair. Favorites that are on the menu all year round are gumbo and spicy, peppered shrimp, and grilled salmon.

Here is where you can find sweet potato bread and hush puppies which you will not find just anywhere in Denver. They have a $5 kids menu. When going to eat at Bang! keep an eye out for the entrance which is located in a narrow alleyway. On nice days the patio is filled with people. This restaurant is located perfectly, it is on a man street but positioned in such a way that there is not much street noise.

Zaidy's Deli

1512 Larimer Street
Denver, Colorado
(303) 893-3600
http://www.zaidysdeli.com/default.aspx

This is a kosher deli that has two locations in Denver the main restaurant is located off of Writer's Square off the 16th Street Mall, the second location is on Adam's Street.

This casual deli is open from 6:30 am to 3:00 pm daily. They offer breakfast and lunch. Check out the box lunches which all come with your choice of potato salad, coleslaw or chips a pickle, fresh fruit, and a homemade cookie. Bread choices are pumpernickel, whole wheat, rye, sour dough, and Kaiser Roll. The most expensive box lunch is $12.95.

Be sure to check out the dessert menu with its pies, cookies, cheesecakes, rice pudding and cookies. While looking for something to drink, try the egg cream.

Steuben's

523 East 17th Street
Denver, Colorado
(303) 830-1001
http://www.steubens.com/

Steuben's is a classic American comfort food. This is a popular restaurant so if expect about a 30 minute wait. If there are 6 or more in your group then call ahead for a reservation. Sundays are the busiest day for this place.

Classic comfort food is what this restaurant strives for. With items on the menu like macaroni and cheese, fried chicken, baked ziti, and flat iron steak among several other choices everyone is bound to find something that will delight their taste buds and remind them of home. Here is another restaurant where you can pick up an egg cream. Steuben's also offers allergy menus for those with food allergies. Be sure to tell your waiter or waitress if you have a food allergy.

Mead St. Station

3625 W. 3nd Avenue
Denver, Colorado
(303) 433-2138
http://www.meadststation.com/

Mead St. Station is a bar that is equipped with a full kitchen. During the day you will find people inside enjoying a meal. At night the place really comes to life with music. Here not only can you get a meal but a drink too.

With an extensive menu you are bound to find food to satisfy what you are craving and all while enjoying music from local bands. The menu has 11 sections. B.Y.O.B. or build your own burger where you can choose the meat, choose the cheese, and even the toppings. The menu also breaks down to sweets, between the bread, greens & things, drinks & beverages, pub grub, sides, soup, specialty burgers, happy hour menu, and signature plates. Here you will find food like Fish n' Chips, Mead St. Nachos, Fried Pickles, Buffalo Chicken Sandwich, and the soup of the day.

As for entertainment there is something different every night. Monday night is Open Mic Night, if you are up for the challenge and want to be put on the list then give Mead St. Station a call. Tuesday night is Rock n' Roll Bingo where music clips and video clips are played with you trying to match them to your card; there are cash prizes. Wednesday through Saturday night has live music.

Osteria Marco

1453 Larimer
Denver, Colorado
(303) 534-5855
http://www.osteriamarco.com/

This Italian restaurant is one of Denver's best fine casual dining restaurants. It will be good for a date, but also good for a quiet family meal. Here you will find a great chef who creates meals. The chef here was cited as one of "10 Denver chefs you need to know". The restaurant offers indoor and outdoor dining. Try the bruschetta or order a pizza. If Italian food is what you crave this is a good place to go. It has an extensive wine list, I am sure the staff would be happy to help if you are not well versed in wine.

Hours are Monday through Thursday 11am to 10pm, Friday and Saturday 11am to 11pm, and Sunday 11am to 10pm. Call ahead for reservations if you want to be sure to have a table. Plates tend to run in the $15 to $25 range.

Places to Shop

16th Street Mall

Downtown Denver
http://16thstreetmalldenver.com/

The 16th Street Mall is in the heart of downtown Denver. It spans 16 blocks. Here is where you will find many stores and some of Denver's best restaurant. Cars are not allowed to drive here so people enjoy the large sidewalks. They can also take one of the free shuttles. Here you can find shops such as Virgin Records Megastore, GAP, and Niketown. Restaurants include Hard Rock Café and Maggianno's Little Italy among many others. This is a wonderful outdoors shopping experience.

Tabor Center

1200 17th Street, Suite 610, Denver, Colorado
(303) 628-1000
http://www.taborcenter.com/

This is a hotel and a shopping experience rolled into one. Come to The Tabor Center if you want to not only shop but eat and relax at a spa.

This modern mall is a wonderful pace to spend a day with some shop therapy. It may not have several stores like other malls but it does have nice boutiques. This is where you will find Secret Garden Florist, Events Dress Boutique and The Shirt Broker. You can also find the Cheesecake Factory in this 3 level mall, office building, and hotel.

Cherry Creek Shopping District

3.5 miles from downtown Denver
http://www.shopcherrycreek.com/

Located in the vicinity of 1st, 2nd, and 3rd Avenues and from University to Steele Street. Here you will find 320 independently owned shops and restaurants. In addition to these are 160 brand name stores. This is the largest, shopping center between San Francisco and Chicago. Here you will find stores in every department. Women's Fashions, Toy stores, maternity, luggage, book stores, and so many other types of shops call Cherry Creek home. The Cherry Creek Bike path leads right to the mall. Check the website for a list of stores though I do not think any shopper would be disappointed here.

Antique Row

400-2000 South Broadway
Denver, Colorado
http://www.antique-row.com/

This is an antique lovers paradise. Here you will find 7
blocks of antique dealers, specialty shops, restaurants and
more. You will find stores that can keep you busy all day.
There are 7 art shops, 11 jewelry shops (which includes
Somewhere in Time), 4 bookstores, and 8 toy, doll and
collectible shops. There are several more stores. After all
of your shopping or even between stores stop in at one of
the 4 restaurants.

South Pearl Street

1569 South Pearl Street
Denver, Colorado
(303) 282-7777
http://www.southpearlstreet.com/index.html

South Pearl Street is a historic shopping district in
Denver. It is also one of the more popular ones. Here you
will find stores such as Gracie's where they provide
unique and affordable clothing and gifts. The Empty
Bottle is a wine shop that specializes in harder to find
wines.

Polkadot is a gift shop where you will find items by a local artist. Hungry while you shop then stop by one of the several restaurants. Budapest Bistro is where you will find Hungarian food. Stop by Lincoln's Roadhouse if you are in the mood for Cajun or Creole cuisine while enjoying some live Blues or Americana music on the weekends. Sexy Pizza is the place in Denver to find New York style pizza. There are several other restaurants for your dining pleasure. Be sure to put South Pearl Street on itinerary.

Lightning Source UK Ltd.
Milton Keynes UK
UKHW02f1852050318
318938UK00007B/1269/P